For the little girl and boy I know
who dream of reaching the stars,
and for you, my dear reader, this one's for you.
JUNIA WONDERS, AUTHOR

Dear Little Friend,
Pick up your favorite brush, chalk, or pastel and draw your life.
It will surely become the most wonderful artwork.
CHIARA NASI, ILLUSTRATOR

Published by Gmür Verlag
Have You Ever Wondered What You Will Be? copyright © Gmür Verlag 2021
Text copyright © Junia Wonders 2021
Illustrations copyright © Gmür Verlag 2021
All rights reserved.

The moral right of the author and illustrator has been asserted.

This is a work of fiction. All names, characters, places, and incidents appearing in this book are the product of the author's imagination or are used fictitiously. Any resemblance to real persons, living or dead, locales, or events is purely coincidental. No part of this work may be reproduced in whole or in part, or stored in a retrieval system, or transmitted in any form or by any means, electronic, mechanical, photocopying, recording, or otherwise, without the prior written permission of the publisher.

ISBN 978-3-907130-17-9

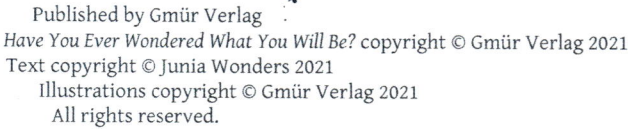

www.juniawonders.com

Have You Ever Wondered What You Will Be?

This inspiring book is a **celebration** of every child's **hopes, dreams,** and **aspirations** for the future, and an **affirmation** of their **boundless potential**.

Have you ever wondered what **you** will be?

When you look in the mirror,
what do **you** see?

Do you **daydream** a lot when you're out on the beach?

Have you ever wondered
what **you** will be?
When you look at the **NIGHT SKY,**
what do you see?

Do you gaze at the stars
and wonder out loud
how to be special,
to stand out in a crowd?

For you may be little,
as little as can be,
but someday you will grow
like a seedling **into a TREE.**

And you may be small,
as small as you are,
but someday **you** will shine
as bright as a **STAR**.

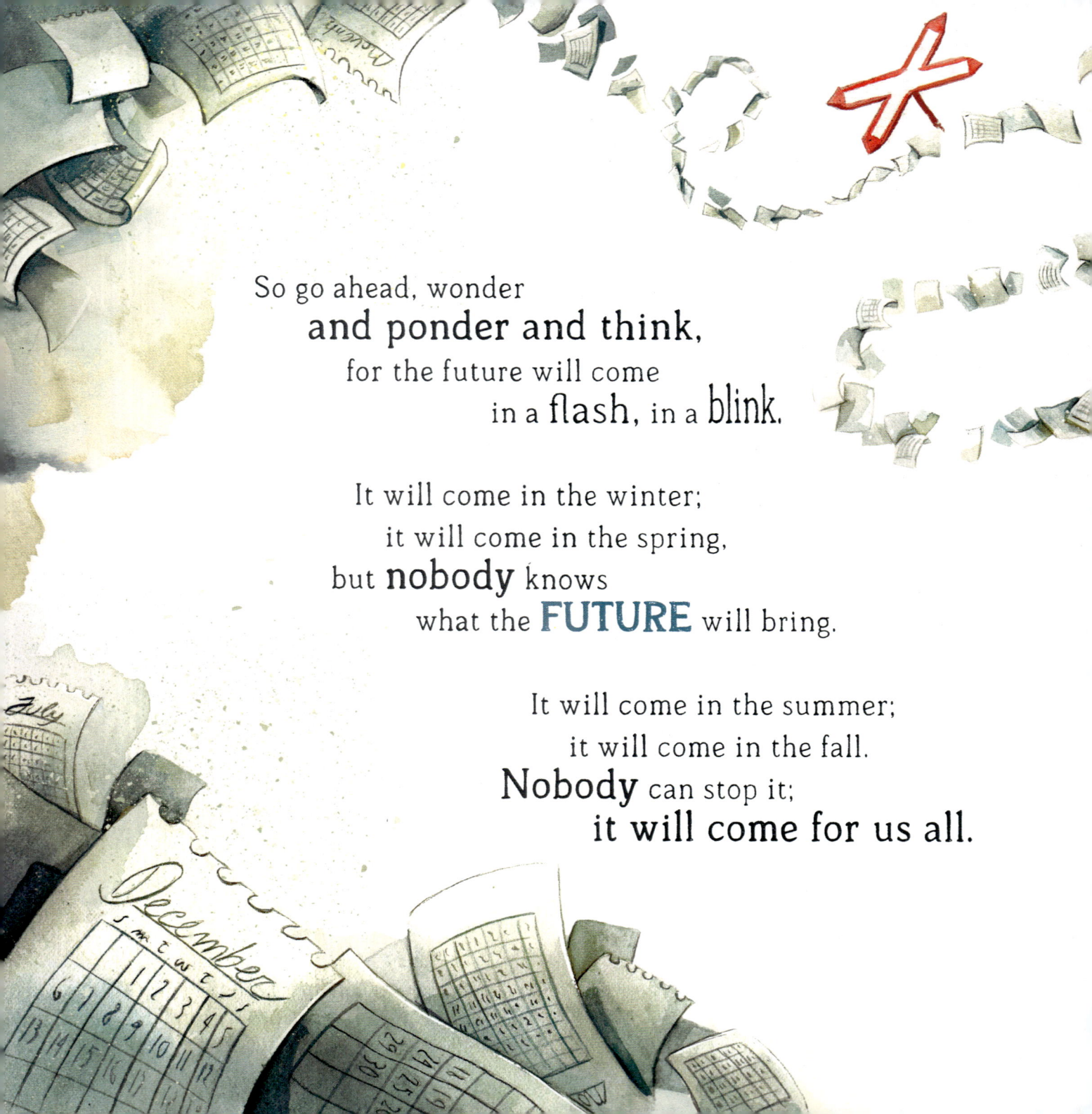

So go ahead, wonder
and ponder and think,
for the future will come
in a flash, in a blink.

It will come in the winter;
it will come in the spring,
but nobody knows
what the FUTURE will bring.

It will come in the summer;
it will come in the fall.
Nobody can stop it;
it will come for us all.

But if you are ready,
as ready as can be,
you will **smile** at the future
and meet it with glee.

You will wake up with **JOY**
and a spring in your step.
You will blossom and thrive
and radiate **pep.**

You will climb atop ladders
and **break through** the ceiling.
You will chart your own course;
you'll be flying, freewheeling.

So it's **NEVER** too early,
it's **NEVER** too soon
to wonder what you will be
and aim for the MOON.

Kid, it's perfectly fine to be a dreamer of dreams as long as you don't end up a schemer of schemes.

And when you find a **DREAM** that's **worth** fighting for, you will jump every hurdle, knock down every door.

For it is through grit and steely **determination** that you'll inch your way closer **to your choice destination.**

And it is through **WORK**, **persistent** and hard, that you'll find your way closer to claim your **reward**.

But **never forget**
 that at times you might FAIL,
for failures and flops
 are part of the tale.

You'll find **yourself** deep
in the throes of despair.
You'll **ponder** and **wonder**
 why life isn't fair.

Well, life isn't always a smooth-sailing ride. There are zigzags and twists, and you can't always glide.

So, if you've ever wondered
what you will be,
the choice is **ENDLESS,**
as vast as the sea.

 Will you be...

an author, a doctor, a chef, a programmer,
an engineer, an accountant, a technician, or a farmer,

 a teacher, an architect, a software developer,
a nurse, a physiotherapist, a lawyer, or a landscaper,

a dentist, a pharmacist, an entrepreneur,
a mechanic, a surveyor, or a restaurateur,

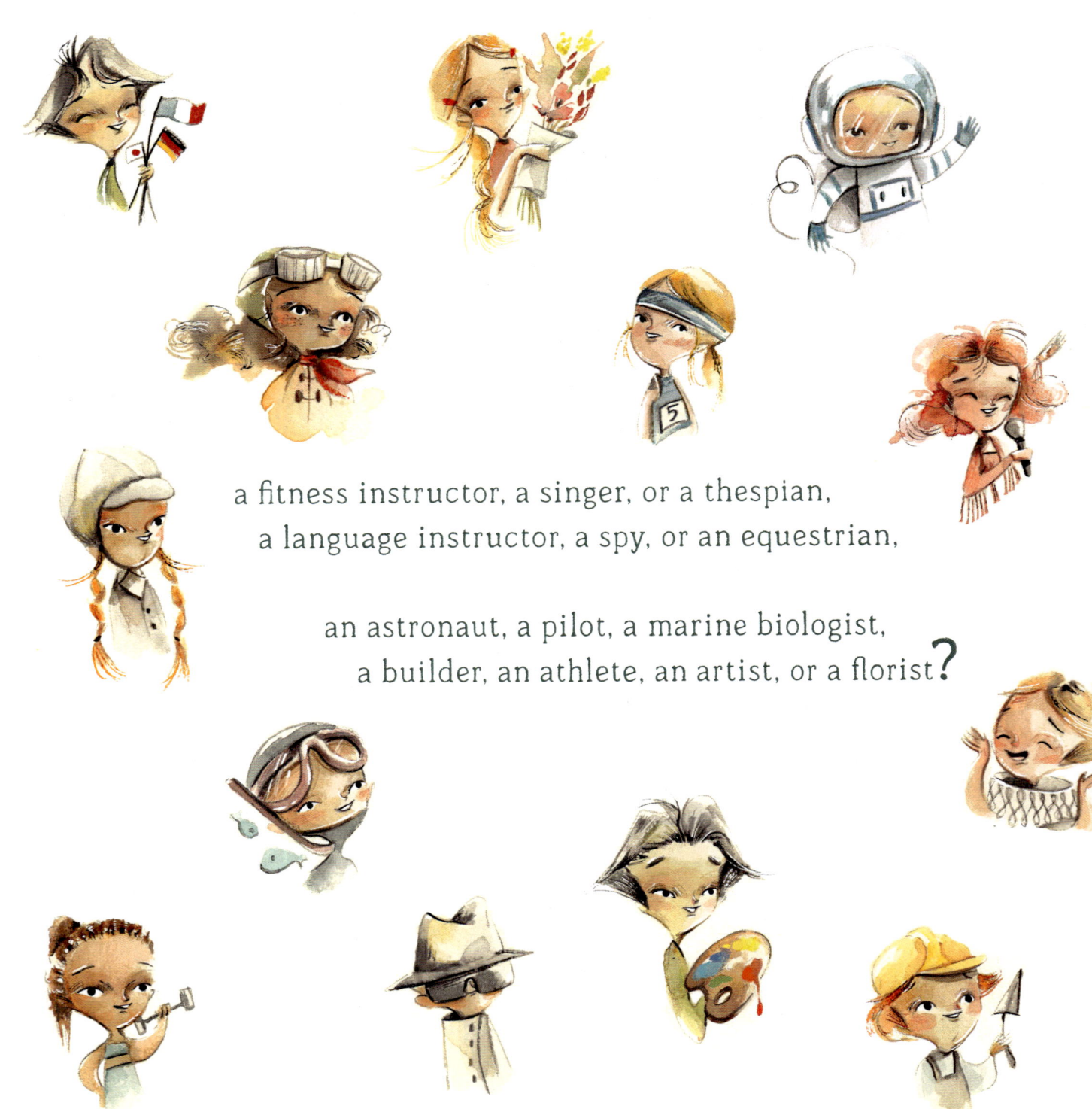

a fitness instructor, a singer, or a thespian,
a language instructor, a spy, or an equestrian,

an astronaut, a pilot, a marine biologist,
a builder, an athlete, an artist, or a florist?

There's more...

an environmental scientist, a wildlife protector,
a product inventor, a professional investor,

a motivational speaker, a writer of rhymes,
a firefighter, a police officer, or a solver of crimes,

a superhero mom, a dad extraordinaire,
or an animal rescuer saving animals everywhere.

Know that this list isn't complete.
Choosing a calling can be a **difficult** feat.

The most important thing
is to look deep inside,
deep in your HEART,
it will help you **decide.**

Whatever path you take,
whichever road you choose,
you will give it **your best shot,**
you've got nothing to lose,

for **LIFE** will just happen
with its highs and its lows.
That's how the world works;
that's how <u>**everything**</u> goes.

Do you see your potential, how special **you** are? Do you know there's no doubt that **you** will go far?

1

2

3

4

5

6

7

8

9

10

11

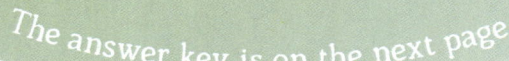
12

13

14

15

16

17

18

Can you name each profession?

The answer key is on the next page.

18

19

20

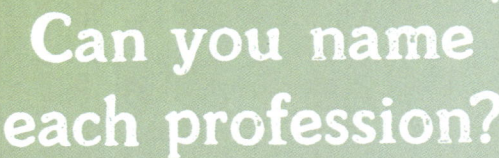
21

Answer Key

1. Teacher
2. Mechanic
3. Motivational Speaker
4. Software Developer
5. Athlete
6. Product Inventor
7. Professional Investor
8. Nurse
9. Firefighter
10. Writer of Rhymes (Poet/Lyricist)
11. Dentist
12. Environmental Scientist
13. Technician
14. Architect
15. Accountant
16. Builder
17. Marine Biologist
18. Artist
19. Wildlife Protector
20. Superhero Mom
21. Chef
22. Language Instructor
23. Astronaut
24. Animal Rescuer
25. Pharmacist
26. Engineer
27. Dad Extraordinaire
28. Police Officer
29. Landscaper
30. Entrepreneur
31. Florist
32. Surveyor
33. Solver of Crimes (Detective)
34. Restaurateur
35. Singer
36. Equestrian
37. Farmer
38. Author
39. Physiotherapist
40. Doctor
41. Spy
42. Pilot
43. Thespian
44. Lawyer
45. Programmer
46. Fitness Instructor

BONUS! Learn positive affirmations for success and the definition of each profession featured in this book by downloading your **free** printable activity sheets at **www.juniawonders.com**.

Books by Junia Wonders

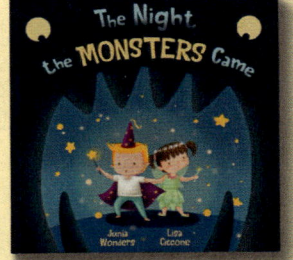
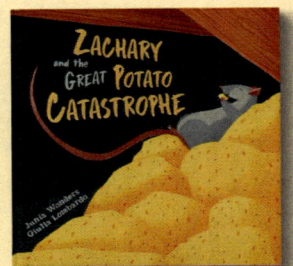

The **paperback** and **hardcover** editions are available on Amazon and Barnes&Noble.

Join *Junia's* VIP list at **www.juniawonders.com** for exclusive giveaways.

Made in the USA
Las Vegas, NV
11 April 2024

88420644R10026